International Newsreel
Underwood & Underwood

1. **Colonel** Lindbergh and Mr. Harry Guggenheim dressed for winter flying.

2. Crew of the "Question Mark," after the world's record of six days in the air, leaving ship at the Metropolitan Airport.

3. Miss Elinor Smith, 17, who made an endurance flight of 13 hours, 17 minutes.

4. Miss Amelia Earhart, first woman to successfully fly the Atlantic, arriving at Southampton, England. L. to R. Lew Gordon, mechanic, Miss Earhart, Wilmer Stultz, pilot.

5. Lady Mary Heath, famous English aviatrix in her Moth plane, in which she made her round trip solo—London to South Africa—welcomed by the Mayor of Miami, Fla.

6. Miss Bobby Trout. 21, of California, who made an endurance flight of 12 hours, 11 minutes.

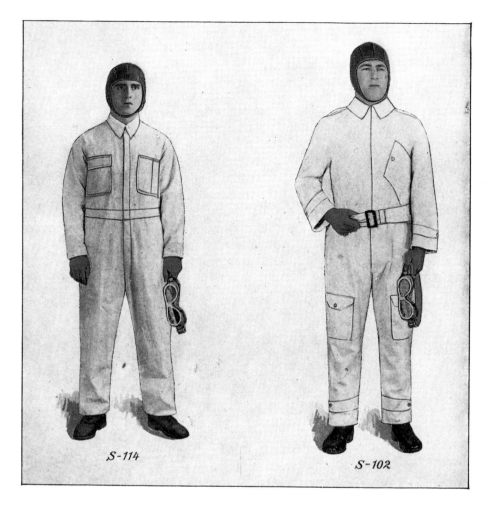

S-114   S-102

S-114. OVERALL SUIT. Made up of white canvas. $5.00

S-102. NAVY CLOTH (KHAKI). Or special white duck cloth. One long patent fastener down front. Tabs on arms and legs. . . $9.00

S-106. RACINE CLOTH SUIT. Overall style. One long patented fastener down front. Tabs on arms and legs. $20.00

S-108. COTTON GABARDINE WATERPROOFED CLOTH. Overall style. Patented fasteners down front, arms and legs. $25.00

ARMY - NAVY SUMMER FLYING SUITS

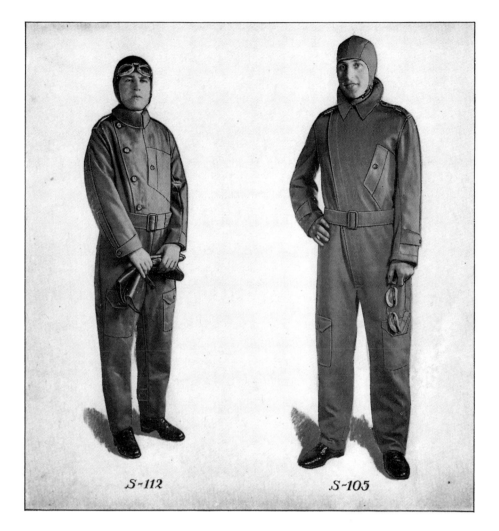

S-112   S-105

S-105. DUCKBACK WATERPROOF CLOTH. Overall style. One long patented fastener down front. Tabs on legs and arms. . . . **$15.00**

S-110. WOOL GABARDINE WATERPROOF CLOTH. Overall style. Patent fastener down front, arms, legs and on pockets. **$35.00**

S-112. WOOL GABARDINE WATERPROOF CLOTH. Overall style. Patent fastener down front, arms, legs and on pockets. **$45.00**

ARMY-NAVY WINTER FLYING SUITS

W-203

W-202

W-201. Twill Waterproof Cloth Shell. Wool cloth lining. Beaverized sheep collar. One long chain; tabs on arms and legs. **$27.50**

W-202. Twill Waterproof Cloth Shell. Beacon cloth lining. Beaverized sheep collar. Five chains on front, arms and legs. **$40.00**

W-301. Waterproof Cloth (Navy) Shell. Rubber sheeting inner-lining, beacon cloth lining. Electrified lamb collar. Five chains on front, arms and legs. **$45.00**

W-203. Duckback Waterproof Cloth Shell. Sheep wool lining. Beaverized sheep collar. Five chains down front, on arms and legs. **$50.00**

W-220. Navy Cloth and Tan Leather Outershell. Woolen blanket lining. Electrified lamb collar. Seven chains down front, arms, legs and pockets. **$65.00**

Illustrated on page 7.

W-280. RUBBERIZED CLOTH OUTERSHELL. Sheep lining; electrified lamb collar; seven chains down front, arms, legs and on pockets. **$75.00**

W-230. ALL-CORDOVAN LEATHER SHELL. Beacon cloth lining. Electrified lamb collar. Seven chains down front, arms, legs and on pockets. **$75.00**

W-303. DUCKBACK CLOTH SHELL. Rubber sheeting inter-lining; clipped sheep wool lining. Electrified lamb collar. Five chains on front, arms and legs. **$75.00**

W-240. NAVY CLOTH AND CHOCOLATE BROWN CORDOVAN LEATHER SHELL. Beaverized sheep lining. Beaverized sheep collar. Seven chains down front, arms, legs and on pockets. **$90.00**

W-270. CORDOVAN LEATHER SHELL. Beaverized sheep lining; electrified lamb collar; seven chains down front, arms, legs and on pockets. **$100.00**

W-211   W-208

W-208. TAN OR CHOCOLATE SHEEPSKIN SHELL. Wool blanket lining; electrified lamb collar. Five chains down front, on arms, legs. **$125.00**

W-305. BEDFORD CORD CLOTH SHELL. Chamois inter-lining. Wool blanket lining. Nutria fur collar. Seven chains down front, on arms, legs and pockets. **$125.00**

W-306. TAN OR CHOCOLATE SHEEPSKIN LEATHER SHELL. Chamois inter-lining, wool blanket lining. Electrified lamb fur collar. Seven chains down front, on arms, legs and pockets. **$150.00**

W-211. CALFSKIN CHOCOLATE LEATHER SHELL. Wool blanket lining. Nutria collar. Seven chains down front, on arms, legs, pockets. **$160.00**

W-220   W-214

W-213. DUCKBACK WATERPROOF CLOTH SHELL. Electrified lamb fur lining. Electrified lamb fur collar. Seven chains on arms, legs and pockets. **$185.00**

W-308. ALL CALFSKIN LEATHER SHELL. Chocolate color. Chamois inter-lining. Wool blanket lining. Nutria collar. Seven chains down front, on arms, legs and pockets. **$200.00**

W-214. TAN OR CHOCOLATE COLORED SHEEPSKIN SHELL. Electrified lamb fur lining. Nutria collar. Seven chains down front, on arms, legs and pockets. **$225.00**

W-215. CHOCOLATE COLORED CALFSKIN LEATHER. Electrified lamb fur lining. Nutria collar. Seven chains down front, on arms, legs and pockets. **$250.00**

W-310   W-311

W-310. Tan or Chocolate Sheepskin Leather Upper Shell. Duckback cloth lower shell. Chamois inner lining; electrified fur lining; electrified fur collar; seven chains down front, arms, legs and on pockets. **$225.00**

W-311. Tan or Chocolate Sheepskin Leather Upper Shell. Bedford cord cloth or jungle cloth lower shell. Chamois inner lining; electrified lamb lining; Nutria collar. Seven chains down front, arms, legs and on pockets. **$250.00**

W-312. All Calfskin Leather Shell. Chocolate color. Chamois inter-lining. Electrified lamb fur collar and lining. Seven chains down front, on arms, legs and pockets. **$275.00**

W-314. All Calfskin Leather Shell. Chamois inter-lining. Nutria fur lining. Nutria fur collar; seven chains . . . **$325.00**

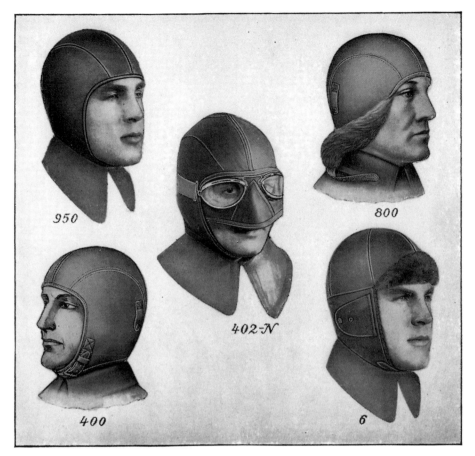

950. Soft Chocolate Brown Leather Summer Helmet. Chamois lining; puff ear pieces exposed; double chin strap. This helmet can also be supplied with the concealed ear pieces at the same price. . **$6.50**

960-C. Same as 950, but with capeskin outershell. . . . **$7.50**

800. Chocolate Brown Soft Leather Winter Helmet. Electrified lamb fur lining. Strap-and-buckle. **$10.00**

400. Navy Winter Helmet. Chocolate brown leather outershell. Beaverized sheepskin inner lining. Chamois lining; leather chin strap. Buckle fastener. Two goggle straps. **$12.00**

402-N. Leather Summer Helmet. Chamois lined; powder puff ear pieces. Two short chin straps with buckles; also patented hookless fastener. With goggles and fastener. Price dependent on goggles.

6. Old Official Army-Navy Winter Helmet. Chocolate brown soft leather. Four-quarter style with visor. Crown lined with chamois. Visor, ear pieces and neck lined with electrified lamb fur. . . **$12.00**

Note: *When ordering helmets, please specify your regular hat size.*

LINED HELMETS

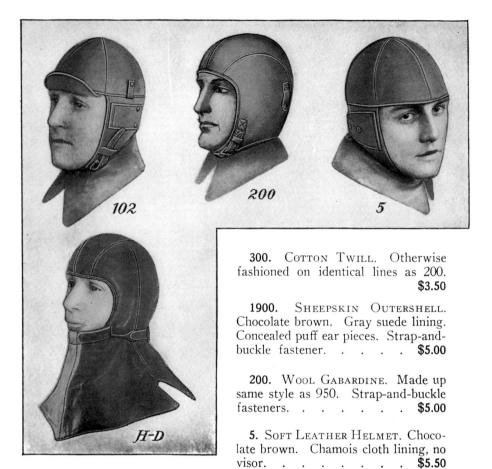

300. COTTON TWILL. Otherwise fashioned on identical lines as 200. **$3.50**

1900. SHEEPSKIN OUTERSHELL. Chocolate brown. Gray suede lining. Concealed puff ear pieces. Strap-and-buckle fastener. **$5.00**

200. WOOL GABARDINE. Made up same style as 950. Strap-and-buckle fasteners. **$5.00**

5. SOFT LEATHER HELMET. Chocolate brown. Chamois cloth lining, no visor. **$5.50**

102. SOFT LEATHER HELMET. Chocolate brown. Chamois cloth lining with visor. This helmet is also very good for motorcycle use. **$6.00**

700. SOFT LEATHER SHELL. Chocolate brown. Pacific Coast style. Leather lining. Fitted with concealed puff ear pieces. . . . **$6.50**

375N. STYLE AS 950. Made with satin lining. Ear pieces exposed or concealed as may be preferred. **$6.50**

950-L. WOMEN'S COLORED HELMET. Supplied on special order only in the following colors—White, Red, Blue, Green. **$10.00**

H-D. HOOD WITH DRAW STRING. Chocolate brown leather. Chamois lining. **$15.00**

Hard crash helmets can be supplied on special order.

UNLINED SKELETON HELMETS

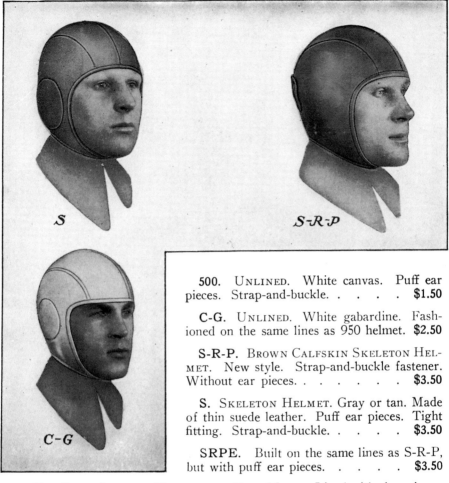

500. UNLINED. White canvas. Puff ear pieces. Strap-and-buckle. **$1.50**

C-G. UNLINED. White gabardine. Fashioned on the same lines as 950 helmet. **$2.50**

S-R-P. BROWN CALFSKIN SKELETON HELMET. New style. Strap-and-buckle fastener. Without ear pieces. **$3.50**

S. SKELETON HELMET. Gray or tan. Made of thin suede leather. Puff ear pieces. Tight fitting. Strap-and-buckle. **$3.50**

SRPE. Built on the same lines as S-R-P, but with puff ear pieces. **$3.50**

50. SUEDE LEATHER HELMET AND FACE MASK. Lined with chamois cloth. **$10.00**

AH. CHOCOLATE BROWN ALL LEATHER HOOD AND FACE MASK. Nutria fur lining. *Special order only. Prices on request.*

GRAF ZEPPELIN first of the dirigibles to cross the Atlantic, on way to Lakehurst.

FACE MASKS

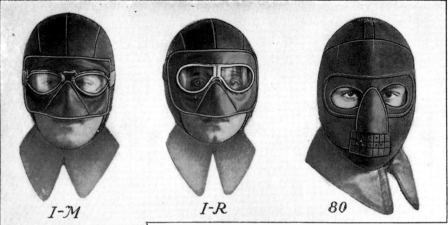

60. SOFT, SMOOTH LEATHER. Glove fastener opening at mouth. Otherwise style as 80, but cheaper leather. Goggles extra. **$4.00**

80. SOFT SUEDE LEATHER. Chamois lined. Holes in mouthpiece for breathing. Braid around eyes to keep goggles from slipping. Goggles extra. **$5.00**

I-R. FUR LINED FACE MASK. Chocolate leather. NAK "Resistal" goggles attached. **$7.50**

I-M. FUR LINED FACE MASK. Chocolate leather. Luxor No. 6 goggles attached. **$15.00**

1. Sir Alan Cobham waves good-bye to "Big Ben". London's famous clock, rising from the Thames, on 20,000-mile-round-Africa flight.

2. Lieut. Benjamin Mendez, Columbian army ace, good-will flyer. with his Curtis-Falcon.

3. National Air Races at Los Angeles. Lieut. Decker banked wide going around the Pylon during the 50-mile memorial race.

OXYGEN HELMETS

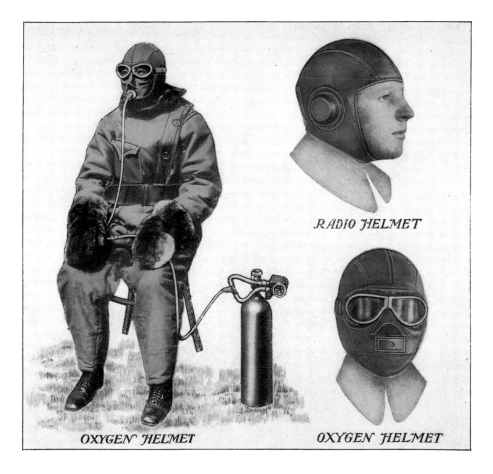

RADIO HELMET

OXYGEN HELMET

OXYGEN HELMET

OXYGEN HELMET. Chocolate brown soft leather shell and face mask. Chamois lining. Face mask sewed to helmet with special opening in mouth for inserting oxygen tubing. Special padding under eyes to make goggles fit closely. Patented chain fastener in the back for opening and closing. *Special order only.* Price without goggles and tubing. **$35.00**

SRH. NEW STYLE RADIO HELMET. Chocolate brown leather. Special molded ear pieces will fit Western Electric 'phones. Two chin straps and strap in rear for adjusting head size. Goggle keepers on side of helmet. **$10.00**

COMMUNICATING HELMETS

W-270

W-310

W-220

78B. THE LATEST COMMUNICATING HELMET.

At Right Showing Inside of Helmet.

A highly efficient speaking device for pilot to talk to passenger, or for instructor and pupil.

Communication in ordinary tones while flying, clearly and distinctly heard above the roar of the propeller. Fully tested and absolutely reliable. Made up of chocolate brown soft leather. Chamois lined with puff ear pieces so constructed that metal ear pieces can be inserted or removed. Single, **$18.00.** Set of 2, **$35.00.**

Complete with two 15-inch flexible metal tubes and one 6-foot flexible metal tube both rubber tipped. Two ear pieces, one "Y" and mouth piece.

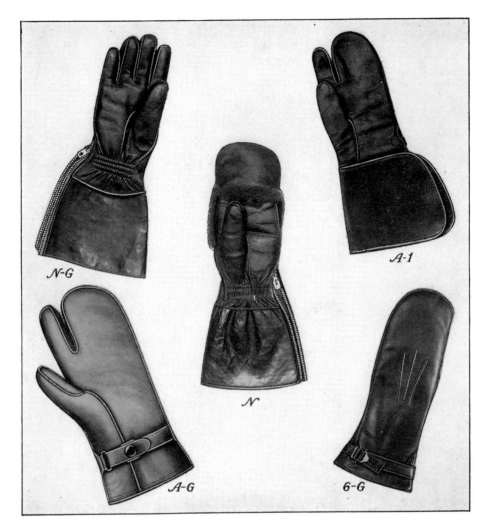

A-G. ONE-FINGERED MITTEN. Wool-lined. Made without the gauntlet. **$5.00**

A-1. ONE-FINGERED MITTEN GAUNTLET. Made up of black leather with wool lining. **$6.00**

6-G. TAN LEATHER MITTEN. Short leather gauntlet with elastic drawn wrist. Wool-knit lining. **$15.00**

N-G. BLACK LEATHER. Same as N, except that it is without mitten attachment. **$17.50**

N. BLACK LEATHER GAUNTLET AND MITTEN COMBINED. Lined with electrified lamb fur. Patented hookless fastener in gauntlet. **$20.00**

ARMY-NAVY GLOVES AND GAUNTLETS

21

A-Back

A-Front

5-G

X-27-Back

X-27-Front

21. Brown Leather—(2-in-1)—Glove. Heavy detachable wool glove inside. . . **$6.00**

X-27. Black Leather Glove. Semi-soft gauntlet with stay reinforcement. Short fingers. Lined throughout with wool fleece. Two adjusting straps on gauntlet. **$12.00**

25. Same as X-27, but made without gauntlet. . . **$12.00**

A. Black Leather Gauntlet-Glove. Fur-lined, with fur-lined flap that can be put back over finger tips, forming finger glove, or mitten. . . **$15.00**

5-G. Tan Leather Glove. With soft leather gauntlet and wool-knit lining. . . **$15.00**

MIRAKEL VEST POCKET BINOCULARS

Mirakel. Equal in Power and Field of View to a 2-lb Binocular.

The Mirakel is so light it can be worn around the neck without case. It is so handily available that the officials of ten government departments use it in preference to heavier binoculars.

5-Power, 5 ounces. **$25.00**

7-Power, 6 ounces. **35.00**

Genuine leather case included.

WOMEN'S ONE-PIECE FLYING SUITS

S-112-L. Wool Gabardine Waterproof Cloth. Overall style. Patent fastener down front, arms, legs and on pockets. . . **$45.00**

W-211-L. Calfskin Leather Shell. Blanket lining. One-piece overall style. **$160.00**

W-310-L. Tan or Chocolate Sheepskin Leather Upper Shell. Duckback cloth lower shell. Chamois inner lining; electrified fur lining; electrified fur collar; seven chains down front, arms, legs and on pockets. **$225.00**

W-311-L. Tan or Chocolate Sheepskin Leather Upper Shell. Bedford cord cloth or jungle cloth lower shell. Chamois inner lining; electrified lamb lining; Nutria collar. Seven chains. . . . **$250.00**

W-312-L. All Calfskin Leather Shell. Chocolate color. Chamois inter-lining; electrified lamb fur collar and lining. Seven chains. **$275.00**

1. Sir Alan and Lady Cobham, on the Thames, about to start their 20,000-mile-around-Africa flight in the "Singapore."

2. The inauguration at Miami, Fla., of the first international passenger and mail service between the United States, Cuba and West Indies. Photo shows—L. to R., Assistant Secretary of Commerce for Aeronautics, MacCracken and Mrs. MacCracken, Miss Earhart, Postmaster General New and S. I. Glover, 2nd Assistant, in charge of air mails.

3. La Nina, the first international service air mail plane to arrive at Havana.

4. Lieut. Ben Eielson and Capt. Sir George Hubert Wilkins, who flew over the Arctic at City Hall, New York.

5. Commander Byrd—A close-up.

Underwood & Underwood

6. L. to R. Oscar F. Grubb, mechanic, and Capt. Hawks at Los Angeles, about to begin their successful trans-continental flight to New York—18 hours, 22 minutes, beating Art Goebel's record by 36 minutes.

7. Lieut. James H. Doolittle, U. S. Army Pilot, winner Schneider cup race, 1925.

8. Art Goebel, first prize winner of $25,000 Dole Air Derby, Oakland to Honolulu, 1927.

9. The Southern Cross.

10. Crew of the Southern Cross flight, San Diego to Australia. L. to R. Capt. Lyon, Capt. Kingsford Smith, Lieut. Ulm, James Warner.

11. Amphibian Biplane arriving in New York with mail from the Ile de France from which the plane took off 500 miles at sea.

L   S

TWO-PIECE SUIT—S. Riding breeches style. Suede leather throughout. Coat—silk lined. Two ample pockets; all-round belt, buckle fasteners. Colors: Tan, Brown, Red, Green, Blue. **$75.00**

TWO-PIECE SUIT—L. Riding breeches style. The coat, made with two large bellows pockets, is tapered from the waist to an extra wide flare at bottom. Colors: Newport Tan, Red, Green, Blue. **$100.00**

With these suits we suggest the WH-15 tan calf leather boot. 15 inches high. Blucher cut, with heavy leather sole and heel. The full bellows tongue extends to top lacing. This style makes an excellent boot for aviation; also for hiking and other outdoor purposes. **$15.00**

WOMEN'S LEATHER COATS

600. **WOMEN'S LEATHER COAT.** Three-quarter length. Wool cloth lining. Two lower pockets and fancy belt. Regular style coat collar.

Supplied in smooth or suede leather. **$25.00**

518-G. **SOFT SHEEPSKIN LEATHER.** Two hip pockets; leather belt. In Tan, Gray, Blue and Black. **$25.00**

702. **FULL LENGTH.** Soft sheepskin leather with two large patch pockets.

Made in Tan, Green, Blue, Black and Red. **$45.00**

MEN'S LEATHER COATS

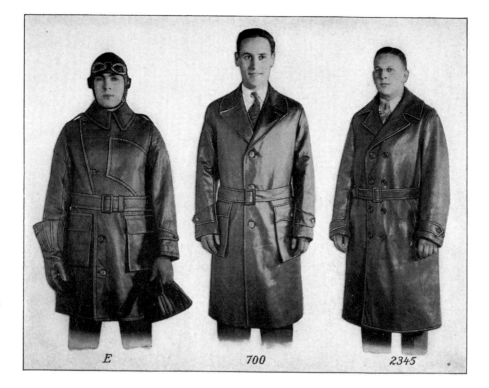

E   *700*   *2345*

RSS. Sheepskin Leather Coat. Chocolate. Thirty-two inches long. Heavy plaid lining; leather facing. **$25.00**

700. Light Weight Sheepskin. Attention is called to two large bellows pockets. Cut knee length with a substantial light wool cloth lining. **$45.00**

2345. Sheepskin Leather Coat. 45 inches long. Wool blanket lining. In Black or Tan. **$45.00**

W. Sheepskin Leather Coat. Chocolate. Forty-five inches long. Reversible. Heavy plaid wool cloth lining; wide leather belt. . **$50.00**

E. English Army Aviators' Coat. Made up of the finest grade of sheepskin. Knee length. Wide leather belt. Two large bellows ,pockets on sides. One very large diagonal breast pocket. Heavy, detachable wool lining over regular lining. **$60.00**

MEN'S LEATHER COATS

RSW

A

RS

601

A. Finest grade sheepskin leather. Wide leather belt; two large bellows pockets on sides, and one large diagonal breast pocket. Detachable wool blanket lining over regular lining.

$50.00

RS. SHEEPSKIN LEATHER COAT. Heavy plaid wool blanket lining. Forty inches long. Chocolate color, wide belt. **$30.00**

RSW. SHEEPSKIN LEATHER COAT. Sheep wool lining, 36 inches long. Chocolate color. **$35.00**

601. MOLESKIN CLOTH OUTERSHELL. Thirty-six inches long. Sheep wool lining; electrified lamb fur collar; four pockets. . . . **$15.00**

MEN'S LEATHER JACKETS

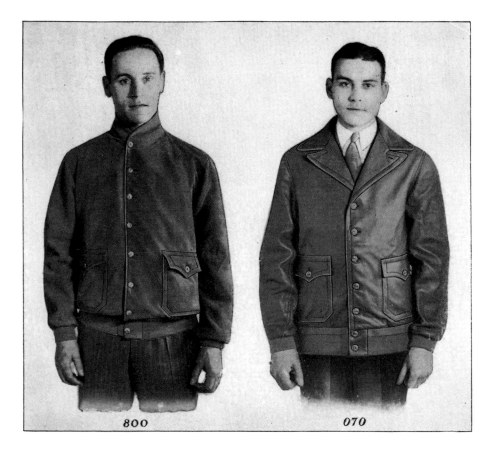

800   070

10N. SHEEPSKIN LEATHER JACKET. Chocolate brown only. Sateen lining; wool knit collar, cuffs and bottom. **$15.00**

RSJ. BLACK LEATHER JACKET. Reversible type. Made with a heavy plaid lining. Leather collar. **$15.00**

800. SUEDE LEATHER SHELL. Sateen lining; wool knit collar, cuffs and bottom. Two lower pockets. In Gray or Sand. . . . **$18.00**

800-R. SUEDE LEATHER SHELL. Reversible. Plaid wool cloth. Two pockets; wool knit collar, cuffs and bottom. In Gray or Sand. **$20.00**

070. IMPORTED GLOVE LEATHER JACKET. Regular coat collar. Wool knit cuffs and bottom strip. **$25.00**

MEN'S LEATHER JACKETS

722   030

010. JACKET. Imported Suede. Lined or unlined. Knit collar, cuffs and bottom. Button front. Two pockets. Gray or Sand. . **$20.00**

030. JACKET. Imported Suede. Lined or unlined. Knit collar, cuffs and bottom. Hookless fastener. Two pockets. **$22.50**

020. NEWPORT TAN GLOVE LEATHER. Knit collar, cuffs and bottom strip. Slide fasteners down front. **$22.50**

722. GLOVE LEATHER. Knit cuffs and bottom strip. Slide fasteners down front. Newport Tan or Navy. **$25.00**

Featuring

the

"Chicago Foam"

INNER LINING

This style of suit was made for the United States Army early in 1925, after exhaustive tests in which its safety and dependability in keeping one afloat was, beyond all doubt, demonstrated.

The make-up comprises wool gabardine of the best grade, with an inner lining of a new patented article known as "Chicago Foam."

It also has patented chain fasteners for quick adjustment in getting in and out.

Prices on request.

As shown in the circle, the wearer of a Spalding Non-sink suit is kept in an upright position while in the water, whether he is conscious or unconscious. This suit will support the weight of a man in water up to two hundred pounds.

SPALDING NON-SINK COATS

NAVY   *EIGHTY*

SPALDING NON-SINK COAT

ATC. OFFICIAL U. S. GOVERNMENT COAT (Patented). Originated and made by us especially for aviators whose duties take them over the water. In event of accident, the coat is guaranteed to keep a man afloat in the water fully sixty hours. It is absolutely waterproof.

Since its introduction during 1917, when the non-sinkable coat was thoroughly tested by government officials in a public swimming tank in Washington and subsequently adopted, it has been used by army and navy fliers.

The outer shell and lining are of waterproofed gabardine. The inner lining is of quilted Ilana-silk or Kapok. Attached are two belts; one

ARMY

passes around the waist, giving a snug fit; the other extends from the middle of the back, between the legs, and is fastened to the inside front of coat, *unnoticeable,* making it impossible for the garment to work up around the body when the wearer is in the water. The non-sinkable coat (patented) is warm and comfortable. It is often used as a short overcoat. **$25.00**

The navy coat has a large Kapok collar. On order only. (*Specify Army or Navy.*)

80. Same as army coat but with sleeves. **$25.00**

***

NOTE: *The crotch belt in both illustrations is shown on the outside of the coat for the purpose of demonstration, but is usually fastened under the coat so that it does not show.*

THE LOS ANGELES FLYING SUIT

The Los Angeles suit comprises three separate articles:

1. Three-quarter length leather coat, a special double-breasted cut, fastening with buttons over right chest. It has two large patch pockets on the sides and one large diagonal pocket on chest, the chest pocket having patented hookless fastener for closing; knit adjustable wristlet lined with best grade Camel's hair cloth.

2. Best grade Angora wool cloth slip-over, having patented hookless fasteners at neck and under each arm.

3. Best grade imported Bedford cloth trousers, lined with papermakers' felt. Patented hookless fastener at ankles and strap and buckle at waist. Built extra large to be worn over regular uniform. **$175**

ARMY-NAVY WADERS

1. WADERS. Mackintosh cloth pants. Shoulder high; with heavy rubber sole. **$16.00**

2. WADERS. Mackintosh cloth pants. Stocking-footed. Worn with O Brogans. . . **$15.00**

3. WADERS. Heavy mackintosh cloth boots. Heavy rubber soles; thigh length. **$12.00**

OFFICIAL AVIATORS' BOOTS

954. MOCCASIN. Fleece lined. $10.00

400. AVIATORS' OVERSHOE. New moccasin style. Leather, fleece-lined. While laced up in front, it has the patented hookless fastener opening at back, contributing ease and speed putting on and taking off. Light, flexible leather sole, sewn on regular moccasin sole. . $17.50

300. AVIATORS' OVERSHOE. Same as 400, but fastener up front only. $16.00

OF. Canvas Upper with Leather Trim. Felt sole with eyelets on side to let water flow in and out. **$7.50**

200. Army Aviators' Overshoe. Moccasin style, made up of the best quality of leather. Fleece-lined. Three strap fasteners. Seamless sole extends up back of heel. **$15.00**

O. Brogans. Heavy leather and canvas; to be worn over stocking-footed waders. Heavy hob nails in soles and heels. Eyelets on sides, allowing water to flow in and out. **$15.00**

O1. Brogans. As O but cheaper leather; canvas and lacing. **$12.00**

300-L. Women's Overshoe. Moccasin style. Patented hookless fastener opening in front. Light, flexible leather sole extends up back of heel. **$17.50**

OFFICERS' HIGH BOOTS

TS. Tramping Shoe. Very durable leather, made up with the moccasin style toe. The shoe is ten inches high. . . . **$12.00**

100. Aviators' Shoe. Substantial leather. Fleece lined. Fourteen inches high. . **$12.00**

AAH. Hunting or Outing Boot. Heavy oil-tanned leather. Laces over instep and side of calf. Sixteen inches high. **$18.50**

600. Hunting Boot. Viscolized leather. Waterproofed. Fifteen inches high. Laced front. **$20.00**

500. Officers' High Boot. Pebbled grain leather. Absolutely waterproof. Fifteen inches high. Laced front. **$25.00**

OFFICIAL NAVY GOGGLE. "Commander." Close-fitting sponge rubber face mask, with extra large curved lenses. Special navy design in bridge and lenses. . . . **$30.00**

MAJOR GOGGLES. Comprises metal frame, with sponge rubber eye-cups. Screw lock, stationary adjustable nose-piece. Curved lenses. **$10.00**

NAK. THE GOGGLE that made "Resistal" famous. Metal frame. Chenille binding; elastic head-band. *Non-splinterable glass.* . . **$5.00**

NAK-V. THE REGULAR NAK, but with special ventilators and triple chenille binding. Former Navy goggle. **$6.00**

NMR. THE REGULAR NAK IN NAVY MASK. **$7.00**

RAV. Same as NAK, but with sponge rubber binding. . . **$6.00**

DG. REGULAR NAK GOGGLES, but lenses colored half green, half white. **$6.00**

WYD. GOGGLES WITHOUT NOSE PIECE. Specially shaped lenses and smaller than the NAK. **$3.50**

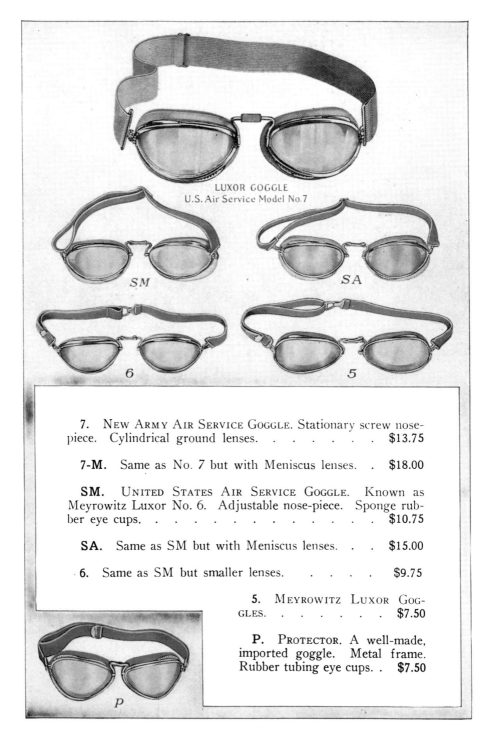

LUXOR GOGGLE
U.S. Air Service Model No. 7

SM

SA

6

5

7. New Army Air Service Goggle. Stationary screw nose-piece. Cylindrical ground lenses. $13.75

7-M. Same as No. 7 but with Meniscus lenses. . $18.00

SM. United States Air Service Goggle. Known as Meyrowitz Luxor No. 6. Adjustable nose-piece. Sponge rubber eye cups. $10.75

SA. Same as SM but with Meniscus lenses. . . $15.00

6. Same as SM but smaller lenses. $9.75

5. Meyrowitz Luxor Goggles. $7.50

P. Protector. A well-made, imported goggle. Metal frame. Rubber tubing eye cups. . $7.50

P

34

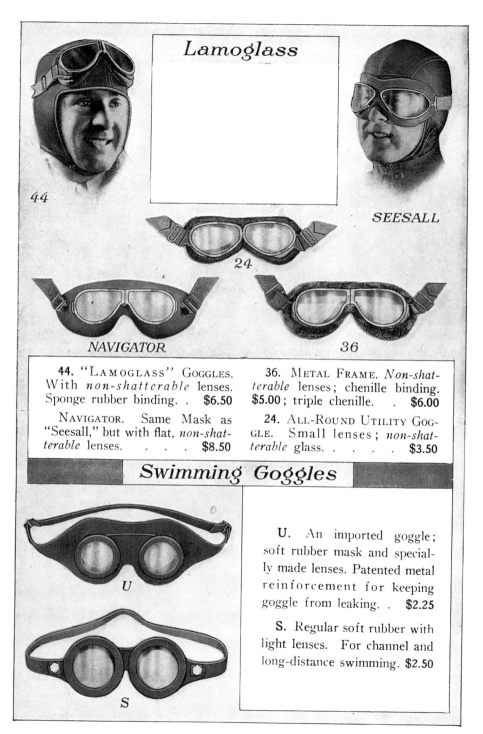

Lamoglass

44

SEESALL

24

NAVIGATOR

36

44. "LAMOGLASS" GOGGLES. With *non-shatterable* lenses. Sponge rubber binding. . **$6.50**

NAVIGATOR. Same Mask as "Seesall," but with flat, *non-shatterable* lenses. . . . **$8.50**

36. METAL FRAME. *Non-shatterable* lenses; chenille binding. **$5.00**; triple chenille. . **$6.00**

24. ALL-ROUND UTILITY GOGGLE. Small lenses; *non-shatterable* glass. **$3.50**

Swimming Goggles

U

S

U. An imported goggle; soft rubber mask and specially made lenses. Patented metal reinforcement for keeping goggle from leaking. . **$2.25**

S. Regular soft rubber with light lenses. For channel and long-distance swimming. **$2.50**

RUSSELL "LOBE" PARACHUTE

The RUSSELL "LOBE" PARACHUTE answers the urgent need of air craft for a practical and efficient life saver.

Designed on aerodynamic principles, it gives positive, rapid opening, even under extremely fouled conditions. There is nothing to get out of order. It operates safely at 100 feet, lessening the low altitude menace. Oscillation is reduced to a minimum, insuring the greatest safety upon landing. It may easily be operated by aerial passengers and aviators, without previous parachute instructions or experience.

STANDARD PARACHUTE, cotton canopy... **$250.00**
    Or silk canopy. **350.00**

OVERSIZE. or 28-foot parachute, cotton
    canopy. **$300.00**
    Or silk canopy. **400.00**

TRAINING OUTFIT. 28-foot parachute and emergency lap pack, cotton canopy. **$500.00**
    Or with silk canopy. **700.00**